How To Make Doll Clothes

A Book for
Daughters, Mothers, & Grandmothers

WRITTEN AND ILLUSTRATED BY

Emily R. Dow

Dedicated to my twin nieces
MARGARET and CARAINN
*For whose dolls these clothes were
designed and made*

CONTENTS

CHAPTER ONE

The Doll Dressmaker

Ways to Use This Book

IT'S SUCH FUN to dress a doll! And if you wish your doll to be as lovely as the one in the shop window, this book is for you. It is for the doll Mother, real Mother, Grandmother, or devoted Aunt who wants to sew doll clothes—for every girl, young or old, loves dolls.

Perhaps you belong to a club, a Girl Scout, Brownie, or Camp Fire Girl troop, or a neighborhood sewing group. If so, you will want to make doll clothes, dress puppets or marionettes, make a masquerade costume, even make simple clothes for yourself, or for a baby brother or sister. You may be too old to play with dolls but want the fun of dressing them for gifts, charity, the church fair, or to send abroad to a little girl who has no doll and would like to know how American boys and girls dress.

This book will show you that it is not necessary to buy a pattern. You will find it more fun to design your own. Anyone who knows how to sew can cut out and make dresses, coats, hats, costumes, and even shoes, from scraps of material found in the house.

If you know how to use a needle and thread, you will be able to

[4]

follow the directions in this book, as they are written for both the young and the experienced sewer.

You may start at the beginning and go right through the book—making your doll family complete outfits. Or perhaps your doll has clothes but you want more for her. Look through the book and choose what you want to make. You may start at any chapter. Some of the clothes are more difficult to make than others, so if you are an inexperienced sewer it is best to start with something simple—like the doll's bathrobe. After you have made one garment and found how easy it is to sew for your doll, you will want to try other patterns.

Use your imagination in trimming and changing the design of a pattern. The pattern for boys' pants can be used to make dungarees—by cutting them ankle length; and a party dress can be made from the pattern for the bride's dress—by leaving out the sleeves and cutting the neck low. If you see a dress on another doll, or even a child, and want to copy it, look through this book and pick out a pattern that is cut basically the same way and add your own details. It's fun to copy dress designs this way.

Tools Needed

A good dressmaker must have the right tools with which to work. Her sewing box should contain needles of all sizes, thread (basting thread as well as thread to match the material), a thimble (be sure it fits), a pair of sharp scissors (keep the point stuck in the hole of a spool of thread when they are put away in the sewing box), a tape measure, and plenty of pins—both safety and straight. A piece of chalk will be useful, but a pencil will do. You will find it easiest to work on a table. A card table makes a good place for cutting patterns. Have a wastebasket near, and make it a habit to toss there the threads and scraps to be thrown away.

Useful Gadgets for the Experienced Sewer

There are many gadgets to help the dressmaker, but these are not absolutely necessary. A person who sews a great deal will find a pair of pinking shears useful. These scissors cut a sawlike edge which will not ravel. An emery bag will help when a needle is old and sticky, for a needle pushed through an emery bag will slip through the cloth more easily. And another useful item is a tape needle to run ribbons, tape, or elastic in garments. But a small safety pin will do the same job.

If you are an experienced sewer, you probably use a sewing machine. Be sure you are using the right length of stitch for each article you make. Small stitches will be needed for fine work, and larger ones to pull up for a gathering. Try out the attachments for tucking, hemming, and ruffling so you can use them in your dressmaking. And if you are lucky enough to own a buttonhole attachment, you will find it is wonderful for making those difficult buttonholes on material that ravels easily.

[6]

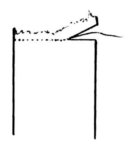

The Easiest Way to Cut and Sew

If your material is wrinkled, be sure to press it before you cut your pattern. Wool material should be pressed with a damp cloth over it. Silk or rayon should be pressed on the wrong side—with a not too hot iron.

Be sure the edge of your cloth has been cut even. If the material has a pattern you can sometimes cut the cloth on an even line, using the pattern as a guide. Some material will tear straight. But when you are working on cloth with neither of these advantages, pull a thread close to the ragged edge (one that will go straight across the material), and cut along this line.

Most of the patterns in this book suggest drawing around the doll. If you are making underwear for her, be sure she wears no clothes when you mark your pattern around her. But when you are planning a dress, leave on her underwear—so the dress will fit nicely over her slip and panties. Use pencil marks or chalk to draw your outlines, and cut after you have removed the doll from the cloth. If there is any question about how large to cut the garment, pin the seams of your outline before you cut, and try the pattern on the doll. It is always better to cut things too large and make them smaller when you find your mistake, than waste material by cutting too small a pattern.

[7]

To adapt the pattern to a child or adult size, take a garment that fits the person and lay it on the material—as you would the doll. (Be sure you have the correct measurements for shoulder seams, sleeve, waist, skirt, etc.)

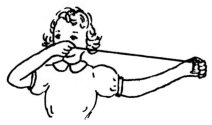

How to Make a Knot in Sewing Thread

Wind the end of the thread over the tip of your finger and hold it there with the thumb of the same hand. Now slip it off by sliding the thumb forward and the finger back. Pull the knot tight.

How to Measure Your Thread

Don't sew with too long a thread—or too short. It should be as long as your arm can stretch—from your nose to your hand.

If you are a young sewer and want to sew the seams by hand with running stitches, make two rows of them. Even with tiny stitches, a single row will break easily and then the seams will pull out. Back stitching is stronger. In fact it is also called "machine stitching" because it looks like sewing machine stitches.

[8]

At the back of the book is a Dictionary of Sewing Terms, with pictures to describe them. Turn to this if there are words in the directions you do not understand. In the last chapter you will also find directions for fancy stitches to use with your doll dressmaking, or to trim baby clothes, bureau scarfs, table covers, and other things you may want to make.

Useful Scraps to Save for Doll Dressmaking

Old cotton socks—make very good shirts and panties. They are just the thing for a small doll's underwear.

Old kid gloves—can be made into shoes and belts.

Old felt—may be used for hats and shoes, as well as trimmings.

Feathers—look nice on doll hats. Squeeze your feather out of a bed pillow. (Do not cut the pillow, but squeeze it with your hand. A feather will usually work out this way.)

Ribbons—of any length may be used. Tiny pieces of different colors can be made into flowers for trimmings.

Lace—should always be saved for trimming—even the smallest bit.

Old curtain material—makes good trimming, and is excellent for a bride's veil. (Especially a silk net curtain.)

Colored yarn—of any length is good for trimmings.

Colored beads or pearls—make good dress trimmings.

Elastic—is needed for doll panties, and even a small piece is usually big enough.

Colored bias binding—makes good edging for many things.

[9]

Embroidery silk—of any color—may be used for trimmings.

Fancy buttons—aside from being useful for fastenings, make good buckles on belts, or trim for a hat.

Small zippers—are useful for snowsuits.

Snaps and hooks and eyes—make easy fastenings.

Fur scraps—of any size are nice for coat and hat trimmings. If the fur has to be cut, have an adult help you. Do not use scissors. Use a single-edged razor blade, cutting the skin on the wrong side. Lay the fur on several thicknesses of paper and cut very carefully, as razor blades are dangerous things to work with.

CHAPTER TWO

Underwear

IN MAKING UNDERWEAR for your doll, always keep in mind the fact that other clothes will go over it. Underwear should not be too bulky and big, or a dress will look queer on top of it.

In selecting material for the doll's underwear, try to find something not too stiff and thick, so dresses will fit well over it. Silk underwear is not necessary under a silk dress. Soft muslin will be just as pretty and fit equally well. It is easier to work on, too.

Underwear does not always need lace for trimming. On the slip, a hem finished with a fancy stitch is very pretty. Try a row of feather stitching around the neck and bottom of the slip, and even on the panties too.

THIS IS FEATHER STITCHING.

Let's start with the panties. Fold your cloth in half and lay the doll (undressed) on the material this way:

[11]

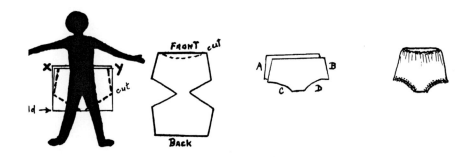

You will find that if you make the panties too short in the back, the doll will not be able to sit easily. When you lay your doll on the folded cloth, be sure the two edges X and Y are higher than the waist. Leave the back of the panties that height, but cut down the top of the front so the center is as low as the doll's waist. Make pencil marks to show where to cut. Then before sewing up the side seams, pin them together and try on the panties to see if you have cut them the right size.

If you are dressing a small doll, you will find it easier to finish the leg bands C and D before sewing up the side seams. A store-bought bias binding makes the quickest finish, but a rolled hem is daintier. Lace may also be added.

On satin or silk an easy finish may be made by using a strip of net for binding. A piece of lace or net curtain works nicely. Fold the net strip in half lengthwise. Next fold it over the edge to be bound—having the rough edges on the underside, and the folded edge on the outside. Baste this in place, then sew along the inside edge—being sure the stitches fasten the binding on both the top and undersides. Use either a machine stitch or a hemming stitch.

The side seams may be sewed together with a machine stitch, back stitch, or two rows of small running stitches.

[12]

Cut a strip of elastic long enough to go around the doll's waist—not tight. Turning the top of the panties down about ¼ inch, sew the elastic to the back of this edge, stretching the elastic as you sew, and having the two ends overlap. This gathers the top.

To make the doll's slip, have the cloth folded in half—with the fold under the doll's neck—and make pencil marks where the pattern should be cut. (See illustration.) The neckline of underwear should be cut low enough to go below the neck of any garment you put on the doll. Gage the length of the slip by the dress length.

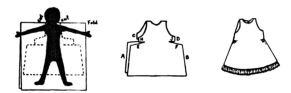

Make a slit down the back to the waistline, and bind this when you do the neck. Sew bias binding around the neck and arm holes—or if you prefer, finish them to match the panties. Do this before sewing up the side seams.

Next sew the side seams C and D, and the seams A and B. E and F are then gathered and sewed to H and J. This will make the skirt full. Turn up the bottom hem and sew on lace for a finish.

One snap will be enough to fasten the back opening at the neck.

[13]

Sew shoulder seams

The doll's shirt should be made from a sock or piece of jersey. For a small doll you can use the top of a sock and you will not need side seams or a hem. If you use jersey, and side seams are needed, it is best to stitch them twice because this material ravels easily. Use two rows of machine stitch, or one row of running stitch and overcast the seams. Instead of binding the neck and arm holes, blanket stitch around them. If jersey has been used, blanket stitch the bottom edge also.

Blanket stitch

CHAPTER THREE

Night Clothes

NIGHT CLOTHES—a nightie or pajamas—should be made from soft cotton cloth, or flannel. If you want a very special outfit, silk crepe may be used. For a bathrobe, use an old flannel blanket if you have one. A small baby blanket of cotton flannel can be bought for almost the same price as new material, and this makes an especially nice bathrobe.

A Nightie for Your Doll

A nightie with a yoke is one of the prettiest patterns to use. It is cut with kimono sleeves, and the bottom of the yoke comes about an inch below the sleeve seam.

Fold a piece of your cloth in half twice: first lengthwise, and then crosswise. Lay your doll on the material with the center of her back coming on the narrow fold, and the back of her neck at the folded corner. Now with a pencil, or chalk, draw your pattern around the doll —showing where to cut under her arm and at the side of her body. Do not draw your pattern too close to the doll or the yoke will be too tight. Mark on the cloth where the side of the doll's neck comes. Then when you remove the doll, cut a rounded neck opening. (See illustration.)

[15]

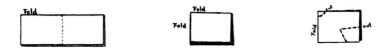

Now open the middle fold of the cloth and cut an opening down the middle of the front—from the neck to the bottom of the yoke.

Sew a bias binding around the neck and at the bottom of each sleeve. Then sew up the side seams of the yoke. Leave the front opening to be bound later.

To gage the width of the skirt, wrap the cloth around your doll once—tight—and measure the cloth so it will be just twice this size. The skirt of the nightie has only one seam and that should be in the front—below the yoke opening. Sew up the skirt seam only halfway —leaving the top part open. Now fold the skirt lengthwise on the seam. Put a pin in the top edge where the back fold comes. (This will mark the center of the back.) Next fold the skirt to find the two points halfway between the pin and the seam. Put a pin in the top at each of these two points. (These mark the sides of the skirt.)

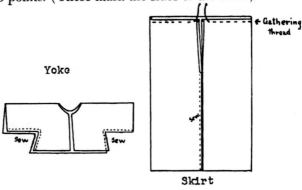

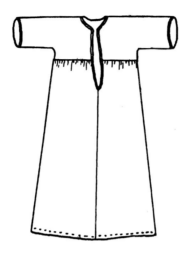

Gather the top edge of the skirt and leave the gathering thread loose. Make a knot in each end of your thread so it will not pull out. Now with the right sides back to back, and working on the wrong side, pin the top of the skirt to the bottom of the yoke. Have the center back pin in the skirt meet the center back of the yoke. The yoke front opening should meet the skirt front opening. The two pins which mark the points halfway between the back and the front should meet the side seams of the yoke.

When these five places are pinned (two front pins, two side pins, and one back pin), gather up the thread at the top of the skirt. Draw it tight until the skirt top is the same size as the bottom of the yoke. If you have made a knot in both ends of the thread, you will be able to pull it from both sides. Wind the ends of the gathering thread over the two pins at the front opening. (This will hold the thread tight and is safer than breaking off the ends and running the risk of losing the gathers.)

[17]

Spread out the gathers between your pins so they will be even. Baste them in place, then sew over the basting to fasten them firmly. When this is done, pull out the basting thread and turn the nightie right side out.

You are now ready to sew binding on the front opening. Use one strip long enough to go around the neck, down the front opening (of both the yoke and skirt), and back up the other side of the opening, to the neck. Have the binding long enough so the ends can be turned under.

Put a narrow hem in the skirt, then sew a snap at the top of the front opening and another at the bottom of the yoke. This will finish the nightie.

Pajamas

This is a pattern for one-piece pajamas. They open down the back and have drop-seat pants.

Cut the front first. Lay your doll with her back centered on the fold of your cloth. (See illustration.) Spread out her leg and arm so

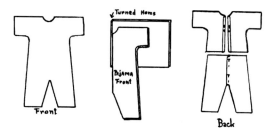

you will be able to draw the width of the sleeve and the size of the leg. Then cut along the lines you have drawn.

To cut the back of the trousers, first pin a fold in the middle of the cloth. This will come between the two legs, reaching from the crotch to the waist, and will make the drop seat full enough to prevent its pulling when your doll is seated. With this fold pinned down, cut the trousers the size of the front. The top should be cut off about an inch below the sleeves.

There will be an opening down the back of the waist. Cut in half the piece you are to use for the waist, and pin the edge of each piece back, as far as you will want the hem of the opening. Lay these two pieces on top of one another and place your folded pajama front on top of this—having the pinned hems together and just under the fold. (See illustration.) Now cut the back of the pajama waist the same size as the front piece. The bottom should be cut off about 2 inches below the sleeves. (This back must be long enough to tuck into the drop seat, so it must go a little below the doll's waistline.)

For the belt, cut a strip of cloth 2 inches wide—narrower if you are dressing a very little doll. It should be long enough to go around the doll's waist loosely and cross over in the front.

[19]

Sew the Pajamas Together in This Order:

First sew the shoulder seams A. Next hem or bind the bottom of each sleeve. Bind the neck, and then hem the waist opening F. Now sew up the underarm and sleeve seams B.

You are ready to work on the trousers. With the fold still pinned in the back, sew the seams on the inside of the legs C. Next pin the two side seams E together—to find the place where the back of the trousers meets the bottom of the waist. Make a narrow hem on the drop seat from this point to the top edge D. Now sew the outside leg seams E up to this hem—up to the bottom of the waist.

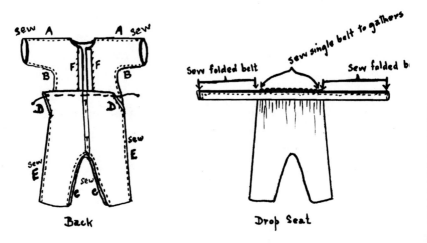

Back

Drop Seat

To finish the top of the drop seat, run a gathering thread in the top, and pull it tight enough to make the seat the same size as the front waist. Fold the piece cut for the belt in half to find the center, and pin this to the center of the drop-seat back. With the right side of the belt and the right side of the trousers together, sew the gathered part to the belt. Fold the two ends of the belt in half—wrong side out—and sew the edges together beyond the gathers of the drop seat and across the ends. Turn the ends of the belt right side out, and hem down the part that comes over the gathers on the inside of the drop seat.

These pajamas may be finished with either snaps or buttons and buttonholes. There should be two fastenings at the back opening—one at the neck and another halfway down to the waist. The belt also needs a snap or button and buttonhole to fasten it in the front.

How to Make a Bed Jacket

The bed jacket may be made of wool cloth, cotton flannel, silk, or quilted material. It is pretty if it is lined. For a lining use silk, muslin, or lightweight flannel.

Cut the jacket with kimono sleeves by folding the material twice —like a hankie. Place your doll on the folded material with the back of her neck at the corner of the folds. Now draw around the doll. (See illustration.) The bed jacket should be loose, so do not draw too close to the doll. The bottom of the jacket should be cut off just below the doll's waist. Cut a slit down the front for an opening.

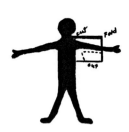
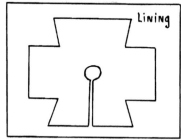

If you do not want to line your bed jacket, just sew up the side and underarm seams, and then blanket stitch around the neck, the end of each sleeve, the front, and the bottom—using yarn of a contrasting color.

If you are lining your bed jacket, the lining should be exactly the same size as the outside. When you have finished cutting the outside, spread it (unfolded) on your lining material, and cut around it.

Before sewing the lining to the jacket, sew up the underarm seams of both pieces. Then pin the two pieces together, wrong side out, and sew the bottom edge of the jacket to the bottom edge of the lining. Next sew the two fronts together. Now turn the jacket right side out. Put the sleeves of the lining through the sleeves of the jacket. You will find that the only unfinished edges are at the ends of the sleeves and at the neck. Baste around these to hold the lining even with the outside, and then sew either a binding or a ribbon (folded in half like a binding) over these edges. At the neck it is pretty to make the binding long enough to tie in a bow and fasten the jacket.

How to Make a Bathrobe

The bathrobe is cut and sewed exactly like the bed jacket, but made long enough to reach the feet of the doll. If a flannel baby blanket or similar material is used, a lining will not be needed.

The simplest way to finish a flannel bathrobe is by blanket stitching around the end of each sleeve, the neck, the front and the bottom, with yarn of a contrasting color.

CHAPTER FOUR

Two Dresses

Kimono-sleeve Dress

ONE OF THE QUICKEST and easiest dresses to make for your doll has kimono sleeves.

To cut the kimono-sleeve dress, fold your cloth in half twice (first crosswise then lengthwise), and lay your doll on the lengthwise fold—with the back of her neck at the folded corner. (See illustration.) Draw the sleeve and side seams, and mark the size of the neck. Take up the doll, and cut your pattern as drawn. You will be cutting through four thickness of cloth. You will also need to cut a slit down the back as far as the waist. Bind the neck opening and this back slit, and bind

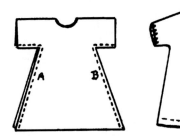

the bottoms of the sleeves. Or, if you prefer, you may blanket stitch them. Sew up the seams A and B, and hem the bottom of the dress. Then sew on a snap to fasten the top of the back opening.

Raglan-sleeve Dress

If you are making a dress for a large doll with a soft body, or a walking doll with stiff arms, you will find the dress with raglan sleeves is the best pattern. This is full around the neck and over the shoulders. It also has deep arm holes so the doll's arms can be slipped into the sleeves easily.

To make a raglan-sleeve dress, the arm hole of the sleeve is cut with the body of the dress. Both the sleeve and dress may be as full as you like, but they should not fit tight. The only measurements you need

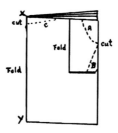

are the length to cut line A (which should be a little longer than the distance from the doll's neck to the underarm seam), and the length of the sleeve or line B (which, if you want a long sleeve, will be the distance from her wrist to her armpit). The cut C should be long enough to go from the top of the doll's shoulder to her chin. Along the fold X to Y, the cloth should be the length you want the doll's dress, with enough extra for a hem.

After you have these measurements, lay your cloth on the table— as illustrated—with two pieces for the dress, folded in half. On these pieces lay the two sleeve pieces, folded in half and marked with the doll's measurements for lines A and B. Cut the line for the arm hole A— all eight thicknesses of cloth. Line B is cut on the sleeve pieces only. Line C is cut to shape the neck.

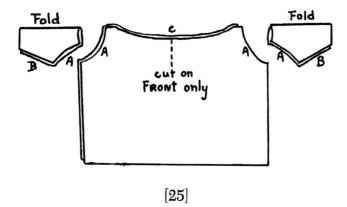

[25]

Gather the bottom of each sleeve into a band, or bias binding. Sew up the side seams of both sleeves and the dress. Then sew the sleeves into the arm holes, with the side seams of the dress and sleeves meeting. Cut a slit down the front of the dress for an opening and bind it.

To finish the neck of the dress, run a gathering thread around the top—starting at one side of the neck opening and running your thread all the way around to the other side of the opening. Draw up the gathering to make it the size of the doll's neck, then sew a bias binding over the gathering—or use a ribbon as a binding and leave long enough ends to tie. You will need no other fastening. Gather the bottoms of the sleeves and bind them with the same trimming.

Now all that is left to finish the dress is the hem at the bottom.

Both the kimono-sleeve dress and the raglan-sleeve dress may be varied in its trimming. After they have been bound, lace may be sewed around the neck and the bottoms of the sleeves. This is especially nice for a white baby dress. Then there are many kinds of embroidery stitches to trim dresses. (You will find some in Chapter Fourteen.) A belt, a sash, or a pocket makes the dress look more grown-up.

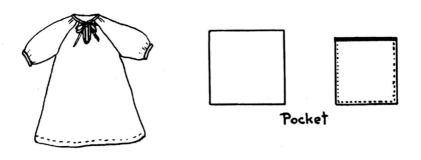

Pocket

[26]

To make a pocket, cut a square of material a size that will look well on the dress. Finish the top edge as you have finished the bottom of the sleeve—with a binding or binding and lace. Turn the other edges under once about ¼ inch, and baste the pocket onto the dress in the position you would like to have it. Two pockets on the skirt look nice. Place them halfway between the center front and the side seam. Have them about one-third of the way down the skirt (measuring from the waist to the hem).

Collars

Another way to change a dress pattern is to add a collar. On the raglan-sleeve dress it is best to put a round collar.

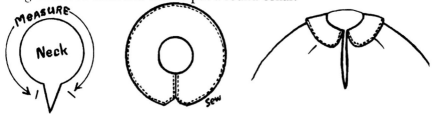

The round collar is cut from a circle. Make a paper pattern first. Draw a small circle, and around this a larger one, and cut them out—cutting a slit from the outside edge to the inside circle. Fit this inside circle to the doll's neck by making a fold at the back if it is too large, or cutting it to fit if it is too small. When you have it the right size, the inner circle will just fit around the neck and the outer edge will lie flat over the doll's shoulders—with the opening coming in the front. Round off the two ends at the front, and cut the collar pattern a width that will look right on the doll. You are now ready to pin the pattern to your material and cut the real collar.

[27]

Have two thicknesses of material under your pattern, for the collar should be double. When you have cut around your pattern, pin the two layers together—wrong side out—and sew around the outside edges. Then turn the collar right side out and sew again around the outside edge—this time on the folded seam.

The collar is now ready to be sewed to the dress. Fold it in half to find the center back, and put in a pin to mark that point. Find the center back of the dress neckline, and put a pin in there. Be sure the pin on the collar and that on the dress meet when you sew the collar to the dress.

Turn under the top neck edge of the collar, and hem it to the neck of the dress on the inside. Be sure the two front points come to the edges of the opening. Next turn down and hem the underneck edge of the collar to the neck of the dress.

The straight collar is cut from one folded piece—the fold on the long side. The width depends on the size of your doll, but for most dolls an inch and a half or two inches is right. Measure around the neck of the dress to find how long to make the collar—adding enough for a seam at each end. Before sewing on the collar, finish the front dress opening with a hem or binding. Then sew up the two ends of the straight collar piece (on the wrong side), and turn the collar right side out. Fold in the front and back edges of the collar about ¼ inch and sew the top edge to the neck of the dress on the inside. Then hem the back edge to the underside.

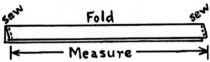

CHAPTER FIVE

Doll Bonnets and Hats

DOLL HATS ARE FUN to make—from material like the doll's coat, pieces of old felt, ribbon, or gingham to match a dress. Fancy buttons, feathers, ribbons, flowers, and bits of yarn make good hat trimming.

Here are some patterns for doll bonnets:

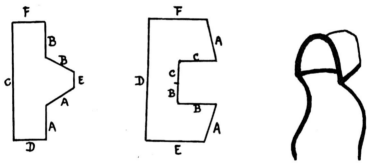

PATTERN 1.   PATTERN 2.

In pattern 1, the side C should be the length around the doll's face. D, E, and F together will go around the neck—sides and back. First join seams A, and then join seams B.

In pattern 2, the side D should be the length around the doll's face. E and F together will go around the neck—sides and back. First join seams A, then gather B to fit B, and C to fit C.

[29]

Finish the face and neck edges with a band of ribbon. (Fold it over the edge and hem it to the bonnet, first on the inside, and then on the outside.) When the ribbon band is sewed to the bottom edge, leave the ends at the front long enough to tie in a bow.

A Baby Bonnet

A pretty baby bonnet can be made from a handkerchief. If it has a fancy edge, that will serve as a trimming, but if it has no trimming, you will probably want to add some lace.

Turn back one edge of the hankie—about half the width of the top of the doll's head—then fold the hankie in half the other way. (See illustration.) Cut off edge A, leaving room for a seam in the center of the back. Cut off the point B. (Pin before you cut, and try the bonnet on the doll.)

Make a French seam at the back. Gather the edges where you cut off the point at B, and draw them up tight on the wrong side. Hem the edge C, when you have had to cut off the trimming.

If you want to add lace, sew it to the front, along the turned-back edge.

Sew several ribbon bows together at the bottom points—each side of the face—leaving ends of ribbon to tie the bonnet.

A handkerchief is large enough to make into an adorable real baby bonnet. Make one for a baby shower.

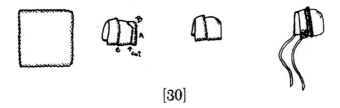

A Scottie Hat

A Scottie hat is easy to make for most dolls. It is cut in two pieces, with a band to go around the crown of the doll's head, and a top piece cut in an oval shape—long enough to reach from the front to the back of the band, and wide enough to fasten to the two sides of this band—with a small fold in the middle.

First cut the head band—the length to go around your doll's head, and allow for a seam as well. The band should be cut double (two pieces). Sew up the back seam of each piece, and then sew the two pieces together by pinning them back to back—wrong side out—and sewing along one edge. Turn the band right side out and sew along the folded seam edge. With two pins, mark the center back—where the seam is—and then the center front.

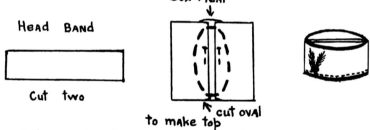

Before cutting the top piece, make a box-pleat fold in the cloth and pin it in place. Put a pin in each end of the fold. Then, with the head band of the hat on the doll's head, lay the pleated cloth on the band—with the box pleat running back to front and the pins of the top meeting the pins in the band. Trim the top oval piece to fit the band, allowing a little to overlap for the seams. Then sew the top and the band together on the wrong side. The pins holding the box-pleat fold should not be removed until the hat is finished.

[31]

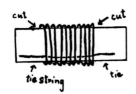

Pompon

How to Trim Hats and Bonnets

A bonnet made of dark material needs two or three pompons to brighten it. These are easily made from bits of yarn. Cut a piece of cardboard 1 inch wide and several inches long. Over one long edge lay a piece of yarn about 5 inches long, and wind over this more yarn of the same color. Ten or twelve winds are enough. Pull together and knot the two ends of yarn over which you made the winds. (See illustration.) Cut the winds of yarn along the opposite edge from the tied side. Now you have a pompon to sew to the top of your bonnet.

If you are putting feathers on a doll's hat, sew a bright button over the stitches holding the end of the feather.

Lucky you, if you have a piece of fur to trim your doll's hat! A strip long enough to go around the crown of the hat, or face the edge of a bonnet, is attractive. But even a tiny piece can be useful. Put a piece—the size of a button—over the sewing that fastens each ribbon tie.

CHAPTER SIX

Coats and Snowsuits

AN OLD WOOL SKIRT, or a piece of woolen coat material, can be made into a doll's coat. If you prefer a snowsuit, use something less heavy—like gabardine, or rayon flannel.

If you are lucky and have pinking scissors, they are a great help when wool cloth is used, because collars, cuffs, and hems can be finished by merely pinking the edge, turning it under ¼ inch once, then stitching it down twice. The first stitching should be close to the folded edge, and the second a little deeper in. If you are working with pinking shears, and plan to make this kind of hem, cut your pattern accordingly. Some wool, such as heavy coating and felt, does not ravel, and this material needs to be turned under only once—even when it has been cut with ordinary scissors.

The Doll Coat

The best coat pattern for a doll has raglan sleeves, because the arm holes are large enough to slip easily over any dress the doll is wearing. To cut this pattern the arm hole of the sleeve is cut with the arm hole of the coat. Both the sleeve and the coat may be as full as you

[33]

like. The only measurements you need are the length to cut line A (which runs from the neck to the armpit of the doll), and the length of the sleeve or line B (which should be the distance from her wrist to her armpit). The cut C should be long enough to go from the top of the shoulder to the chin. X to Y should be the coat length, with enough extra for a hem.

After you have these measurements, lay your cloth on the table—as illustrated in Figure 1—with two pieces for the coat, folded in half. On these pieces lay the two sleeve pieces, folded in half and marked with the doll's measurements for lines A and B. Cut the line for the arm hole A—all eight thicknesses of cloth. Line B is cut on the sleeve piece only. Line C is cut to shape the neck. D is the coat side seam. (Cut only where the dotted lines are shown—following the illustration in Figure 1.)

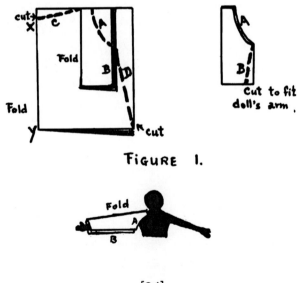

Cut to fit doll's arm.

FIGURE 1.

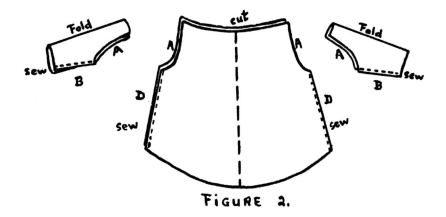

FIGURE 2.

Turn the bottom edge of the sleeve under ¼ inch, and stitch this hem down twice. Sew the seams D and B (see illustration in Figure 2). Next sew the sleeves into the arm holes—matching A on the sleeve to A on the coat. Do not cut the front opening until this is done. Most wool ravels easily so it is best to have as few raw edges as possible exposed while you are working on the garment. Now cut the front opening and turn up the bottom of the coat—finishing it like the bottom of the sleeve.

Each side of the front opening should be faced with a strip about 1 inch wide and as long as the coat—before the hem is turned up. This facing should match the coat in material or, if you are using another color for the collar of the coat, perhaps you would like to make the coat facing of that material. If possible, cut these strips so one long side of each is on the selvage. Otherwise, make a narrow hem along one long edge of each strip. Pin and sew one of these strips to each side of the front opening—the long, unfinished edge should be along the coat edge,

[35]

and the wrong side of the material out. Now turn the strip inside the coat and sew along the folded seam—down the front opening. At the front of the neck, where the facing comes, turn the coat material under ¼ inch, then fold the facing in to match and sew the folded edges together. This will make a finished edge at the neck where the two fronts will overlap when the coat is fastened. At the bottom of the coat, turn the facing in and sew it to the hem.

To make the coat collar, a paper pattern should be drawn first. Draw a small circle, and around this a larger one, and cut them out—cutting a slit from the outside edge to the inside circle. Fit this inside circle to the doll's neck by making a fold at the back if it is too large, or cutting it to fit if it is too small. When you have it adjusted to the right size, the inner circle will just fit around the neck and the outer

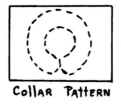

Collar Pattern

edge will lie flat over the doll's shoulders. Round off the two ends at the front, and cut the collar pattern a width that will look right on the doll. You are now ready to pin the pattern to your material and cut the real collar. Because coat material is heavy, the collar will have no lining and it will be cut from one thickness of cloth.

Hem the collar as you did the bottoms of the sleeves. Then before you sew it to the coat, run a basting thread around the neck of the coat, and try it on the doll. Pin the front together as it will be worn, and draw up the basting thread, gathering the neck to the correct size. While the coat is still on the doll, lay the collar in place and put pins in to mark where the front points of the collar come. Take off the coat and sew on the collar. Lay the right side of the collar on the wrong side of the coat, with the neck edges meeting, and the front of the collar at the pin marks on the coat. Sew the two pieces together, close to the edge. Then turn the collar to the right side of the coat, and sew again along the neck seam.

Sew a snap fastener at the neck closing, or make a buttonhole. (Buttonholes will make it more like a store coat, but unless you are experienced at making buttonholes, or can use a buttonhole attachment on the sewing machine, you will find working on wool difficult.) Sew two or three buttons along the front edge, just below the neckline. These buttons are just to trim the coat.

If you are an experienced sewer, and if you have a piece of fur, you may want to put a fur collar on your doll's coat. Fur should never be cut with scissors, so have an adult help you cut it with a single-edged razor blade. The skin should be cut on the back side, and one narrow strip long enough to go around the doll's neck loosely is all you need. Sew the fur on the right side, fastening one edge to the neck of the coat —on the inside. Use a catch stitch for this.

How to Make a Snowsuit

Perhaps you would like a snowsuit for your doll. Use cloth of one color for the suit, and a contrasting color for the hood lining. Plaid cloth makes a nice lining, if you have it. If you are an advanced sewer and know how to sew on a zipper, you may want one for the snowsuit. It should be long enough to reach from the neck to the crotch of the doll.

The snowsuit is cut like the front of one-piece pajamas. (Turn to Chapter Three for the pajama pattern.) For the pajama the side seams are straight, but for the snowsuit, shape the side seams so the suit will not fit the doll too tightly over her hips. (See illustration.) Fold the

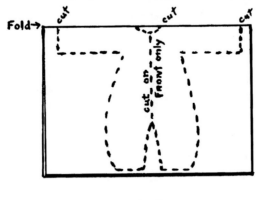

[38]

cloth in half at the shoulders and cut the back and front together. Cut a slit all the way down the middle of the front for an opening.

Finish the front opening before sewing up the seams of the suit. If you want to fasten it with snaps, you will need to sew a facing of the same material (or material like the lining of the hood) to the two sides of the front opening. Have the facing wide enough so one side can over-lap the other. The snaps are sewed to this.

The front may also be fastened with a zipper. First baste back the edges of both sides of the front opening about ⅛ inch. Then pin and baste these to the sides of the zipper, with the folds lapping over the metal to meet. Stitch about ⅛ inch from the zipper.

If you follow these steps in order when you are sewing the snow-suit, you will find it simplifies the work:

Have the front opening completely finished and fastened before you sew the rest of the suit.

First hem the ends of the sleeves. Then sew up the underarm and side seams, but do not sew the seam at the crotch yet.

Next finish the bottom of each leg. Baste a hem at the bottom edge, and sew this to a strip of elastic. Have the elastic long enough to go around the doll's ankle loosely. (Before cutting it, pin the strip of elastic and see if it will slip over the doll's foot.) Stretch the elastic as you sew the hem to it. This will gather the material and make it possible to stretch the opening.

Sew up the seam at the crotch.

You are now ready to make the hood. To do this, lay a piece of your material on the doll's head and wrap the edge around her face, bringing the sides together under her chin. Mark the point where the sides meet with pins. With the material still over the doll's head, pin the cloth together at the back of the doll's head—to show where the seam will go. Put in more pins to mark where to cut the material around the doll's neck. Take off the cloth and cut out the hood, outside the pins—allowing enough for the seams and hem.

If you would like a pixy-style hood, do not cut the back where you put in pins, but shape the hood to a point, and make the seam from the back of the neck to the point. (See illustration.)

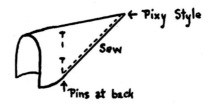

If you are lining the hood, lay the hood you have cut on the lining material and cut around it. Sew the face edges together—wrong side out. Then sew up the back seams of each piece separately. Slip the lining into the outside part of the hood. Now with the outside of the hood against the right side of the suit, pin and then sew the bottom edge of the outside hood to the neck of the suit. Then turn the bottom edge of the lining under and hem it to the neck.

If you have no lining for the hood, after you have made the back seam (where you put in pins), turn the hood right side out. Now pin and sew the neck edge to the neck of the snowsuit—with the right side

of the hood against the right side of the suit. Turn the edges under inside the neck and hem them down.

A piece of velvet ribbon may be used to face the front edge of the unlined hood or, if the hood is cut big enough, it may be hemmed around the face.

Sew a tiny bell to the pointed hood, and you will have a real pixy cap.

A Bunting

Every baby doll should have a bunting. It can be made from a cotton baby blanket, a piece of wool coating, or flannel.

The pattern for this bunting is very simple—a large bag with a little hood at the top and an opening down the front. The bag is cut in one piece, with a fold over the shoulders.

Fold the material in half and lay your doll with her shoulders slightly below the fold. Cut the bag around her—allowing room for her to stretch out her arms and legs. Cut the neck opening by making a slit along the fold under the doll's neck. Take up the doll and cut an opening down the center of the front, from the middle of the neck opening to the bottom of the bag.

Sew a binding of the same material along both sides of the opening. Make it wide enough to extend about ½ inch beyond the edge. When the bottom of the bag is sewed, these bound edges will overlap.

If you are an experienced sewer you may want a zipper down the front of your bunting—instead of a binding. In that case, baste back both edges of the opening about ⅜ inch. Then pin and baste these to the sides of the zipper with the folds lapping over the metal to meet. Stitch about ⅛ inch from the zipper.

Now sew up the sides and the bottom of the bag, making the seams on the wrong side. Then turn the bag right side out and it will be ready for the hood.

The hood is made like the one on the snowsuit. Turn to page 40 and follow the directions given under the picture of the hood. Make it pixy style or plain.

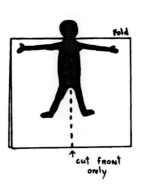

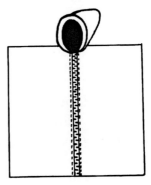

CHAPTER SEVEN

A Jumper and Pinafore

EVERY LITTLE GIRL'S DOLL should have a jumper or pinafore. The jumper may be made of cotton or wool cloth, but a lightweight cotton material should be used for the pinafore.

The Jumper

The belt of the jumper should be cut first, from a strip of material long enough to go around the doll's waist and cross over to fasten. Measure it over the underclothes. The width will depend on the size of the doll, and it will be double. Fold the material in half lengthwise, before you cut it the width for a belt.

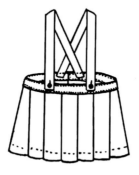

[43]

Measure and cut another piece of cloth for the skirt. This should be wide enough to go around the doll's waist twice, and long enough to reach from her waist to below her knees. Allow enough to turn up for a hem.

Make a narrow hem halfway down the two ends of the skirt piece. This will be the back placket. Next lay the belt strip (unfolded) on a table, and fold over one long edge and the two ends about ¼ inch. Now beginning at the center of the belt, and the top center of the skirt, pin the skirt to the long, folded edge of this strip in pleats. Fold a box pleat in the center front, and make single pleats on either side. They should be small and even. Plan them carefully so the pleated material will fit the length of the belt. After you have worked out the size the pleats should be, and have put in pins to hold them, baste the skirt to the belt. Fold over the top edge of the belt ¼ inch, then fold the belt in half lengthwise and baste it to the top of the skirt pleats. Now sew the belt close to the lower edge and along the two ends.

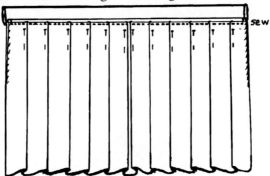

Next sew the back seam of the skirt up to the placket. Then you are ready to put in your bottom hem. You will also need to sew a snap fastener at the belt closing in the back.

The skirt is ready for shoulder straps. Cut these so they will be the width of the belt when finished. They should be long enough to go from the bottom of the belt in front, over the shoulder of the doll, cross in the back, and go down to the bottom of the belt in back. Cut two of these straps. Fold each strap in half—lengthwise and wrong side

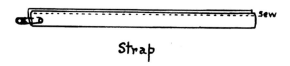

Strap

out—and sew the long outside edges together. Now turn the straps right side out. (To do this, fasten a safety pin in one end and run it down inside the strap, pushing it through until it comes out the opposite end, bringing with it the cloth turned right side out.) Next turn in both ends of each strap and hem them.

Put the skirt on your doll, and pin one end of each of the straps to the skirt belt in back. (The ends should go inside the skirt and a little to the sides of the back placket.) Cross the straps at the doll's back, and pin them together where they cross. Run a strap over each shoulder and down under the skirt belt in front. Put a pin in where the strap meets the top of the skirt.

Take the skirt off the doll and sew the straps where they are pinned to the skirt in back, and at the crossed place. On the front ends of the straps, sew on snaps so they will fasten to the belt (either on the underside or the outside).

If you are an experienced sewer, you may want to make a buttonhole in each end and sew a button on the skirt band where the strap will fasten.

[45]

How to Make a Pinafore

A pinafore is usually made of lightweight cotton cloth—organdy, dimity, dotted swiss, or muslin. Most pinafores have ruffles of the material, embroidered edging, or ruching over the shoulders. The embroidered edging from the bottom of an old slip makes a good ruffle.

Ruching

Cut the skirt wide enough to wrap around the doll's body twice—because you want it full. Make it long enough to reach from the doll's waist to the bottom of her dress. (A pinafore is usually shorter than the dress it goes over, so this will give you room for a hem at the bottom.)

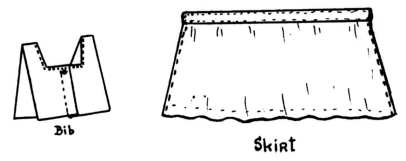

Bib

Skirt

Make a narrow hem down the two back edges. Then hem up the bottom of the skirt. Next run a gathering in the top. Start with a knotted thread and leave the thread long, tying another knot in the end when you finish. In this way you will be able to pull up your gathering thread to make the skirt fit the belt.

[46]

The belt is made of a folded strip of the material—long enough to go around the doll's waist and cross over in the back to fasten. It should be measured over the underclothes. The width will depend on the size of the doll. Fold the material in half lengthwise before you cut it the width of the belt.

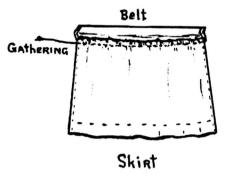

Now lay the belt strip on a table and fold over one long edge and both ends, about ¼ inch. Next, with the skirt wrong side up, pin it to the long folded edge of the belt. First pin the top of the hemmed ends of the skirt to the turned down ends of the belt. Then draw up the basting thread in the top of the skirt so that it is the length of the belt. Spread the gathers out evenly, and pin the top in several places along the belt edge. Baste along the gathers. Then turn the top of the belt over ¼ inch and, folding it in half lengthwise, baste it to the top of the gathered skirt, on the wrong side.

The bib should be cut as wide as the doll measures across the shoulders, and long enough to reach from her waist in front, over her

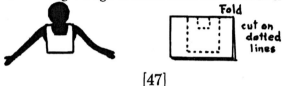

[47]

shoulder to her waist in back. Fold your material in half at the shoulders and cut a square neck—cutting the front and back of the neck halfway down to the doll's armpit and leaving the width of the shoulders at both sides.

Now working on the wrong side, pin and then baste the front of the bib to the front of the skirt. (Fold the front bib in half and put a pin in the center. Do the same with the skirt, and have these two pins meet when you fasten the bib to the skirt.) Pin and then baste the back of the bib to the back of the skirt, having the top and bottom plackets meet. Now sew all around the belt, close to each edge. Remove all the bastings, and then sew snaps to the top of the bib opening and at the belt opening in the back.

Cut a slit down the middle of the back of the bib. This will be the back opening. Hem both sides of this opening. (These sides will overlap a little to fasten the pinafore. This will make the back of the bib narrower than the front, but the doll's back is narrower than her front.)

Make a narrow hem around the neck and along each side of the bib. Before you turn the corner with your neck hem, cut a small slit in each corner. This will make it easier to turn a smooth hem.

After the bib has been hemmed, pin your ruffling or embroidered edging to the back of the outside edges. Baste, and then sew it in place. (Some ruching comes sewed to a band, but if the inside edge is not finished, your pinafore will look neater if you take the time to sew a bias binding over the gathered edge before you sew it to the jumper.)

CHAPTER EIGHT

Daughter and Mother Outfit

IT'S FUN TO HAVE a Daughter and Mother twin outfit. This is an easy one to make. Perhaps you would like it for yourself and your doll, or you and your mother can make outfits together.

The Skirt

To make the skirt, turn to the directions for the jumper on page 43, because this skirt will be made the same way. The only differences are that the material is gathered to the belt instead of being pleated, and there are no shoulder straps. In this pattern, the belt can be wider than a jumper belt.

[49]

Use a bright printed cotton and make the skirt full. If the material is a plain color, without a pattern, use the width for the length of the skirt. A figured material will have to be cut in two or three strips the length you want the skirt. Seam the strips together before you gather them to the belt band.

The Peasant Blouse

This is a good blouse to make for your doll to wear under a jumper or pinafore. It can be cut in larger sizes too, so it will go with the skirt of a Mother and Daughter outfit.

Use a thin cotton material—dimity, muslin, organdy, or dotted swiss. For the neck and sleeve binding, ribbon or cotton bias binding looks nice.

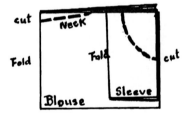

The blouse is made with raglan sleeves, and it is cut like the pattern for the raglan-sleeve dress on page 24. If you do not understand the above illustration, turn to the directions for measuring and cutting the raglan-sleeve dress and cut your blouse exactly the same way— only of course make it blouse length instead of dress length. A blouse should reach a little below the waist.

To finish the blouse, first gather the bottom of each sleeve into a binding, then sew up the sleeve seams. Next sew the blouse underarm seams. Now stitch the sleeves into the blouse—with the underarm sleeve seam meeting the blouse seam. Bind the front opening, then run a gathering thread in the neck—gathering up the top of each sleeve with the neck. Draw up the gathering thread to make it the size of the doll's neck, then sew a bias binding over the gathering. Leave long enough ends to tie and you will need no other fastening.

CHAPTER NINE

Shoes, Slippers, and Stockings

IT IS HARD TO FIND ready-made shoes to fit every doll, but if you have an old leather glove or felt hat, and a bit of yarn, you can make shoes for your doll. Old socks can be made into doll's stockings.

A doll's shoe is so tiny it is easily lost when it falls off. The shoe with an ankle strap is therefore the best kind for her to wear. These shoes are made to fit either foot, so cut two just alike to make a pair.

Lay a piece of felt—or leather—on the table, and draw around one of the doll's feet. Then cut your pattern (as illustrated), around the foot outline. The sides should be high enough to fold up to the top of the doll's ankle. The strap from A to D should be long enough to reach from the back of the foot, around the ankle, and cross in the front. The piece E should be cut half the size of the foot.

If you are making the shoe of leather, sew it together with very strong thread the same color. A felt shoe may be sewed with bright yarn. Take small stitches over the edges—overcasting.

First find the center front (on the rounded edge) of the piece E, and pin it to the center front of the shoe. Then run a gathering thread in the front edge of the shoe, and draw it up to fit the top piece you

[52]

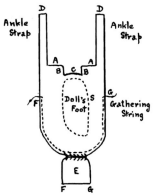

will sew to it. (F on the top piece should meet F on the shoe; and G on the top piece should meet G on the shoe.) Now take small stitches and overcast the two pieces together, sewing around the front of the shoe from F to G. The straight edge F to G may also be overcast with the same yarn, or it may be left plain.

Cross the straps over the doll's ankle and sew a snap to the two ends D to fasten them.

Now overcast the edges A together, then overcast B to the back of the shoe C.

A Shoe Cut in One Piece

This shoe pattern is good for leather, but it may also be used with felt. It can be made to fit a real baby.

The illustration will show you how to draw the pattern, and if you follow the directions carefully, you will know how to measure the doll's foot.

[53]

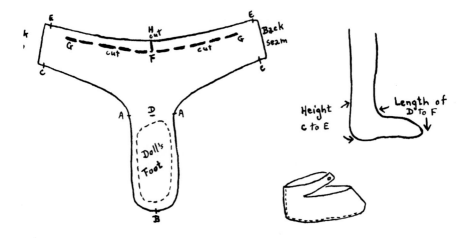

Cut the pattern large enough to allow for seams beyond the foot. The length from A to B should equal that from A to C. Leave enough material beyond the points C and E for the back seam of the shoe. The distance from C to E should be the height you will want the shoe in back—including the width of the strap. D to F is the top of the shoe, and this should be the length from the tips of the toes to the opening. The top edge E to E must be a little longer than the distance around the ankle—allowing enough more for the ankle strap to cross and fasten, as the cut line G to G makes the ankle strap.

This shoe is sewed on the inside with small machine stitches made close to the edge, down the back seam and then around the sides and back of the foot. When this is done, turn the shoe right side out and put it on the doll's foot to measure where the strap fastening should come. The strap may be fastened with a snap, or a very small button and buttonhole.

[54]

How to Make a Slipper

A doll's slipper may be made from felt, or flannel like her bathrobe. It should be sewed with yarn.

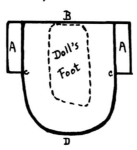

Draw your pattern around the doll's foot. Notice that on the illustration, section A is half the length of the foot. C across to C should be wide enough to wrap over the top of the doll's foot and allow a seam beyond. The rest of the pattern should be cut at an equal distance from the foot outline, except at the back B. This should be in line with the back of the foot.

To sew the slipper together, first fold it in half lengthwise. Then overcast together the edges at the back B. Overcast the edges of the front together from C to the top of the toe D. Now all that is left to do is to finish the edge of the cuff of the slipper A. Blanket stitch around that.

These slippers can be made for a real baby or an adult. They make good Christmas presents. Make a paper pattern by drawing around the bare foot of the person you want to fit.

A Doll's Stocking

Stockings can be made from your old socks, and they are very simple to cut and sew. If possible, use only the top of an old sock, because that will start you with a finished top edge for the doll's stocking. The stocking is made with only one seam—going up the back. Fold your material in half, and cut the stocking the desired length, rounding it at the toe end. Be sure to cut the stocking wide enough to go around the doll's leg, and allow enough for a seam as well.

Sew up the seam of the stocking on the wrong side, and overcast the edges of the seam to prevent raveling. Turn the stocking right side out and it is ready to put on.

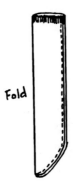

CHAPTER TEN

Sunsuit, Sunbonnet, and Overalls

In summer your doll will need all three of the articles of clothing described in this chapter. The patterns for the sunsuit and the sunbonnet can be used for a real baby. Make these of cotton cloth—crinkle crepe trimmed with bias binding is good. For the overalls, striped cotton seersucker works nicely. Corduroy may be used, but it is hard to work with.

The Sunbonnet and Sunsuit

The sunsuit is cut in one piece—except for the two straps. Make these double (with a fold on one long side) and cut them so they will be half the width of the doll's shoulder when finished. They should be long enough to reach from a little below the top of the sunsuit in front, go over the shoulders, cross in the back, and go a little below the doll's waist in back.

Fold each strap in half lengthwise, with the wrong sides out, and stitch the two long edges together. Fasten a safety pin in one end and run it through the strap, bringing it out the other end to turn the strap right side out. Turn in the ends of each strap and hem them.

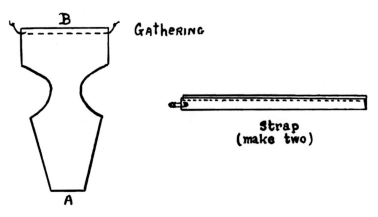

In measuring the size to cut your sunsuit, lay the doll on the folded material and mark around her—to show where her waist, hips, and crotch come. Before cutting, study the illustration carefully. The front

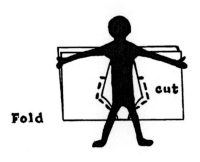

[58]

piece goes into a bib above the waistline, so cut only the pantie part with the cloth folded. Then open the fold and cut the bib on the front. Cut the back piece waist length. The top of the bib A should be a little narrower than the doll's chest. The back of the waist B should be wide enough to gather a little, yet reach across the back and under the front edges to fasten.

 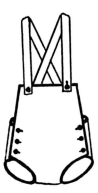

Gather the top of the back and draw up the gathering thread, so that the back is just wide enough to come around and fasten under the front at each side. Next bind all around the suit with a contrasting binding.

The illustration shows where to put buttons and buttonholes, and if you are an experienced sewer, you will want to fasten the suit that way. However, snaps may also be used—three at each side of the pantie.

After you have sewed the fastenings to the sunsuit, put it on your doll and pin on the straps. One end of each strap should be fastened to the waist in back—on the inside of the suit. Then the straps are crossed, go over the shoulders and down to the front of the bib—overlapping enough to fasten. After you have pinned them the right length, sew the straps at the back, and put snaps or buttonholes on the front where they fasten to the bib.

In making the sunbonnet, cut the visor double. You will need to measure around the doll's face to find the length to make the straight edge A to B. The front edge is curved.

The back of the bonnet is made with buttons or snaps to fasten it in shape. The length of the bonnet from front to back, E to F should be the distance from the doll's forehead, over her head, and down to the back of her neck. The front edge E should be the same length as A to B on the visor. Lines C, D, and F are fastened together to go around the sides of her neck. F goes across the back of her neck. So measure the doll to see how long to make these edges. (Measure loosely because you must allow enough so the bonnet will fasten together.)

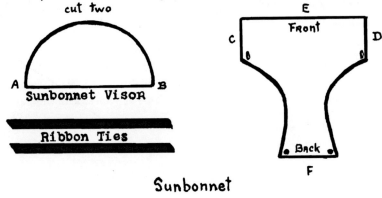

Sunbonnet

[60]

When you have cut out these pieces, lay one of the visor pieces on the bonnet piece—with the right sides together, and the wrong sides out. Pin edge A to B along edge E. Now lay the other visor piece on the back of the bonnet piece—with the right side of the visor piece against the wrong side of the bonnet piece. Pin edge A to B along edge E. Next sew close to edge E, fastening the two visor pieces to the bonnet. Then turn the visor pieces forward (over the seam you have made) so they lie flat together at the front of the bonnet. Pin and then baste around the visor edge to hold them together.

Now sew a bias binding (to match the sunsuit) all around the edge of the bonnet and visor.

If you are an experienced sewer you will want to fasten your sunbonnet together with buttons and buttonholes. The illustration shows where to make these. The buttonholes go on the back corners of the two sides C and D, and the buttons on the two corners of the edge F. If you are using snaps to fasten the bonnet, sew the top of each snap to the underside of the corners on C and D. The bottom of each snap goes on the outside of the edge F.

Sew two tying ribbons—one at each side of the bonnet—at the point where the visor is attached.

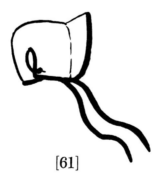

[61]

The Overalls

The front and back of the overall pants can be cut together. Before cutting, the back piece should have a fold pinned down the middle so the seat will be full enough. (See Figure 1.) After the fold has been pinned, place the back piece of material on top of the front piece, and lay your doll so the fold is in the middle of her back. Now draw, and then cut, around her two legs and hips. Allow plenty of room for seams, and also remember that the pants legs should not be tight. Cut the top off at the waist.

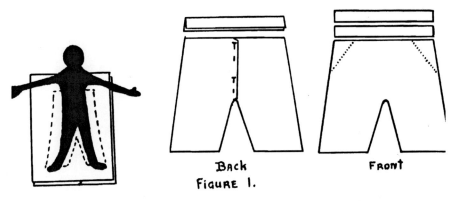

BACK   FRONT

FIGURE 1.

This overall pattern has a pocket on each side of the front. So turn both top corners of the front piece back—with a diagonal fold. Stitch along the edge of each fold once. Now cut two squares of material to fit over each triangle and space left by turning the corners down. (See Figure 2.) Sew the two edges of each turned down triangle to the corresponding two edges of each square. This makes the pockets.

[62]

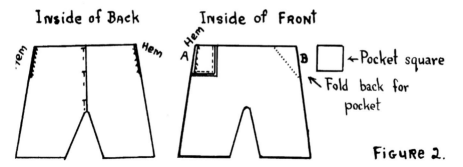

Inside of Back

Inside of Front

Hem

Hem

Hem

A

B

☐ ←Pocket square

↖ Fold back for pocket

FIGURE 2.

Make a narrow hem on the side edge of the pocket square, and a hem the same width and length down each side of the back piece of the pants. Seam the sides of the front and back together below these two hemmed edges. Do not sew up the inside leg seams until the cuffs have been put on.

The cuff is made by sewing a long, straight, folded strip of the material to the bottom edge of each pant leg—like a wide binding. Have it wide enough so it can be turned up to make the cuff. After this wide binding has been hemmed to the bottom of the leg, turn it up along the hemmed edge and pin it in place—on the outside of the pants. Then sew the inside leg seam. (This will hold the cuff so it will not turn down when the doll wears the overalls.)

Inside

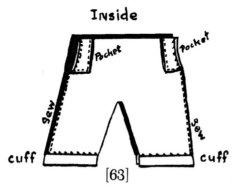

Pocket

Pocket

sew

sew

cuff

cuff

[63]

The overalls should have a bib top. Cut this a little narrower than the front waist of the pants, and long enough to sew to the waist and reach to the armpits, with enough extra for a hem at the top. Make a narrow hem on each side and a larger one at the top. Then sew the bib to the top of the trousers.

Cut two strips of cloth to make a front belt. They should be long enough to reach across the front waist, and about 1 inch wide. (The width depends on the size of the doll.) Turn under the edges of each strip about ⅛ inch. Baste one strip to the front of the overall waist, and one to the back of that strip. (The bib will be between.) Stitch them in place.

To finish the back waist, first unpin the fold in the center of the back. Then run a gathering thread in the top of the pants. Try on the overalls and gather up the back thread to make the top just long enough to reach across the back and fasten under the two ends of the front belt. When you have fitted the back this way, take off the overalls and sew a binding of the same material to this gathered top. (Make the binding a little longer than the gathered top of the pants, and a little more than twice the width of the front belt. Turn under and baste all the edges of the strip about ⅛ inch, then fold the material in half lengthwise.)

Fasten the two side plackets with snaps, or buttons and button-holes. The front should fasten over the back.

The two shoulder straps should be the same width as the belt of the

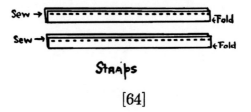

Straps

[64]

overalls. Cut them double, with a fold on one long side, and allow a little for the seam on the opposite edge. They should be long enough to reach from a little below the top of the bib in front, go over the shoulders, cross in the back, and go a little below the doll's waist in back.

Fold each strap in half lengthwise, with the wrong sides out, and stitch the two long edges together. Fasten a safety pin in one end and run it through the strap, bringing it out the other end to turn the strap right side out. Turn the ends inside the straps and hem them.

Sew the straps to the belt in back—on the inside of the waist band. Now put the overalls on your doll and fit the straps to her. Cross them behind and bring them over her shoulders and down to the bib in front. They should overlap the hem on the top of the bib.

The straps may snap to the bib. But if you wish you may make a buttonhole in each end and sew a button to each corner of the bib where the strap will fasten.

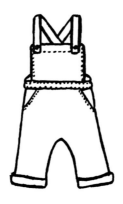

CHAPTER ELEVEN

Dressing a Boy Doll

MAKING CLOTHES FOR a boy doll is no more difficult than sewing for a girl doll. Cotton jersey can be used for a little suit of shirt and pants; or, if you like, he can have a gingham blouse to wear with the pants. Save some of the pants material for a beanie, to complete the outfit.

The Jersey Suit

Starting with the jersey shirt, it is best to cut your pattern in four pieces. The back and front may be cut together but there should be a seam over the shoulder because one shoulder will be finished with an opening—so the shirt will slip over the head easily.

Lay your doll on two folded pieces of material—with the middle of the doll's back on the folds. (See illustration.) Cut the shirt pattern around the doll, leaving plenty of room for seams at the side and shoulder, and rounding out the bottom of the arm holes A. Be sure to cut the bottom of the shirt long enough so it will tuck into the pants after it is hemmed.

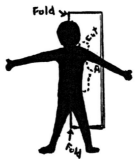

In cutting the sleeve, fold the material in half and lay it beside the arm hole of the shirt. Then cut the top of the sleeve to fit the arm hole. Make the sleeve long enough to reach from the shoulder to the wrist—allowing for a hem. Shape the sleeve so it will fit the wrist at the bottom. Finish the bottom of the sleeve with a hem or binding. Sew the top into the arm hole.

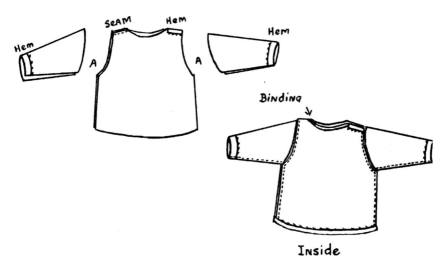

[67]

Now sew up one shoulder seam. The other is finished with a hem on each edge and a snap to fasten the front to the back. After these seams are finished, bind around the neck with a strip of bias binding cut from the same material. (Directions for cutting a bias bind are given in Chapter Fourteen.)

Now all that is needed to finish the shirt is to sew up the side and sleeve seams, and hem the bottom.

The Pants

The pants are cut in two pieces, with a seam down the center of the front and another down the center of the back. Cut out the pants by laying the doll on two pieces of folded material, with the folds along the side of the leg. (See Figure 1.) Make the front seam long enough to fit the doll comfortably—reaching from the waist to at least an inch below the crotch.

Cut halfway down both side folds and bind the openings. Sew the center front and back seams, and bind the legs of the pants. Then sew up the seams at the crotch. (See Figure 2.)

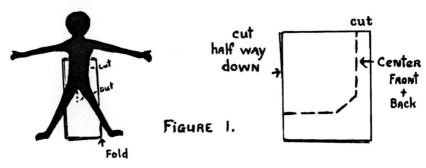

FIGURE 1.

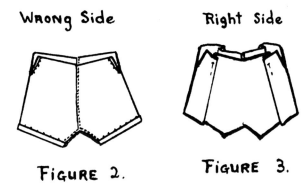

WRONG Side   **Right Side**

FIGURE 2.   **FIGURE 3.**

Try the pants on your doll, pinning the two side openings closed. Make a small tuck on each side of the front seam, and on each side of the back seam. Pin these tucks so the top of the pants will fit the waist. (See Figure 3.) Unpin the sides of the pants, and take them off the doll.

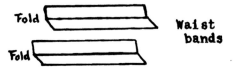

Fold   **Waist**
Fold   **bands**

Now make a belt—or wide binding—to fit the front and another to fit the back of the waist. (See Chapter Fourteen if you do not know how to sew a binding.) Cut the binding strip a little longer than the top of the pants—so the two ends can be turned in—and when you sew the binding to the pants, keep the tucks in them.

[69]

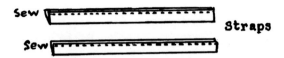

Sew Straps

Make two shoulder straps by cutting two strips of the material—long enough to go from the belt in front, over the shoulders, cross, and fasten to the belt in back. They should be cut twice the width of the doll's shoulders. Fold these two strips of material in half lengthwise and stitch the long edges together on the wrong side. Turn them right side out by fastening a safety pin in the end and running it through the strap.

Try the pants on your doll and fit the straps. Sew one end of each strap to the back of the waist band on the wrong side. Then cross the straps, carry them over the doll's shoulders, and mark the place where they will fasten to the front waist band.

Turn in the front end of each strap and hem it. Then sew the top of a snap to the back of the end, and the bottom of the snap to the waist band—where the strap will fasten. On the front of the strap, directly over the snap, sew on a button.

If you are an experienced sewer, you may want to fasten the front of the strap to the waist band with a button and buttonhole. The button will go on the waist band, and the buttonhole in the end of the strap.

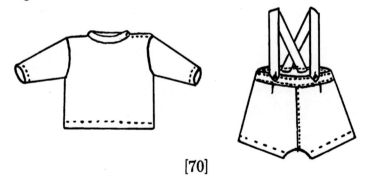

[70]

The Gingham Shirt

The gingham shirt is cut from a folded piece of material—in one piece, except for the collar and the front facing. Place the doll on the folded material—with the doll's neck resting on the fold—and draw around the doll. Mark where to cut the neck opening, the bottoms of the sleeves, and the sides (allowing for the seams). Cut off the bottom of the shirt just below the doll's waist. Then cut an opening down the middle of the front. Lay one of the front edges of this opening on two thicknesses of cloth and cut a facing. Round it to fit the neck and make it about an inch wide all the way down the front. (Wider if the shirt is to fit a large doll.) For the collar, cut a straight piece two inches wide (this width too depends on the size of the doll), and make it the same length as the neck opening—from the front, around the back, to the front again.

To sew the shirt together, first hem the bottom of each sleeve. Next sew the facing to the front opening. This is done by laying the facing on the front with the wrong sides out, and sewing close to the front edge. Now fold the facing back against the inside of the shirt and sew along the fold. The other edge of the facing should be hemmed. Sew the side seams next. Then hem around the bottom of the shirt.

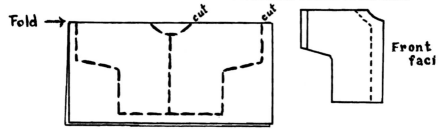

Fold →   cut   cut

Front
faci

[71]

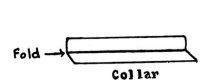

Fold →

Collar

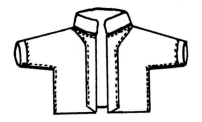

Wrong side out

Now you are ready to put on the collar. Fold the collar strip in half to find the center back, and put in a pin to mark it. Then fold the neck edge of the shirt in half—front to back—and put in a pin to mark the center of the back. Next pin the collar strip around the neck of the shirt—with the right side of the collar against the wrong side of the shirt —starting at the center back where the two pins should meet. Sew on the collar strip, close to the neck edge. (The collar will be a little longer than the neck edge.) Now turning the long edge of the collar under about ⅛ inch, and folding the collar in half lengthwise, hem it to the neck. Turn the front ends of the collar in—making them even with the front opening—and hem them.

Snaps, or buttons and buttonholes, may be used to fasten the front opening.

[72]

How to Make a Beanie

To find the size to cut your beanie, measure the crown of your doll's head where the bottom edge of the cap will come. Divide this by five, and add a half inch to the number you have. This will be the width of the bottom edge of each piece (C to B). Cut it the shape illustrated, with the height of each piece the length from the top of the doll's head to the point where you measured for the bottom edge. Cut five pieces.

Now sew the edge from A to B of one piece to the side A to C of the next piece. Continue sewing one piece to another until you have all five sewed together.

Cut a bias strip of the same material ½ to ¾ inch wide, and use this for binding the lower edge of the beanie. (If you do not know how to cut a bias binding, turn to Chapter Fourteen where it is explained.)

Turn your beanie right side out, and sew a button to the top where the five pieces come to a point.

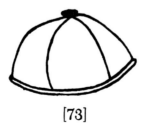

CHAPTER TWELVE

Masquerade and Puppet Costumes

HERE ARE TWO FANCY dress costumes. They are fun and not difficult to make. The Clown suit can be cut to fit you, your doll, a Puppet or Marionette. (A one-piece costume, with long sleeves and ankle-length pants, is good for a Marionette because it will cover the parts that move.) The Ballet dress can be made for both you and your doll. Remember this chapter when you are planning for a costume party.

The Clown Costume

For the Clown suit use two different colors of material. One-half the costume is one color, and the other half another color. To cut the suit, fold a piece of cloth of one color in half lengthwise and lay the doll on it, with the fold at the center of her back. Mark around the doll to show where to cut. The suit should be very baggy, so do not cut close to the doll. Cut the pants leg off below the doll's foot, to make it loose when it is hemmed and gathered around the ankle. Round out the arm hole. (See illustration.)

Now cut along the fold to make two separate pieces—one for half the back, and one for half the front of the suit. Cut the other half of the Clown suit from another piece of folded material (a different color). Use the first part you have just cut for a pattern.

Next cut the sleeves—one to match each side of the suit. Lay a matching piece of cloth, folded in half—with the fold at the top—beside the arm hole. Cut the top of the sleeve to fit the hole. The sleeve should be very wide all the way down to the bottom. (To make it baggy.) Cut it long—below the doll's hand—because it will be gathered at the wrist and hemmed.

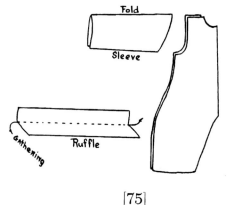

Sew the shoulder and middle front seams. Sew the back seam halfway up from the crotch—leaving it open from the waist to the neck. Sew in each sleeve. Then sew the side seams and the inside leg seams.

Turn up a wide hem at the bottom of each leg, and at the bottom of each sleeve. Stitch these hems twice—once at the top of the hem, and again ¼ inch down from this. Using round elastic, run a piece in each hem—between the two rows of stitching. Use a safety pin to run the elastic through the hem. Tie the elastic tight enough to just fit around the ankles and wrists.

Finish the neck of the suit with a ruffle. Make it in two colors, twice the length around the doll's neck, and twice as deep as the ruffle on the sleeve. (Measure around the neck and cut one piece this length from material of each color, then sew the two pieces together to make a long strip.) Hem both edges, and run a gathering thread through the center, lengthwise. Draw the string up so the ruffle will fit the neck of the suit. Around the neck of the suit, turn a small hem down on the right side. Then make a narrow hem on the two edges of the back opening. Now stitch the ruffle to the neck hem—stitch through the middle of the ruffle, along the gathering.

Sew small snaps at the back opening to fasten the suit.

[76]

How to Make the Clown Hat

To make the Clown hat, first cut a half circle from paper. To do this, first cut a piece of string about 1½ inches longer than you want the height of the hat to be. Tie a pencil in the end. Now with one finger holding the other end of the string to the paper, stretching the string as far as it will reach, and holding the pencil straight up and down, draw the pencil around your finger making a half circle. Cut out the half circle and lay the pattern on either color of your material. Cut the cloth to fit the paper.

Lay the cloth on the paper pattern with the wrong side on top, and sew the cloth to the paper along the straight edge of the half circle. Turn the cloth right side out and smooth it down over the other side of the paper. Then baste the paper and the cloth together along the curved edge. Now fold the straight edge in half (A meeting B), and slide edge B along edge A until the hat fits the doll's head. Hem the outside straight edge to the hat—from the bottom edge to the point.

Make a small ruffle like the one you put around the neck of the Clown suit. Sew this to the bottom edge of the hat.

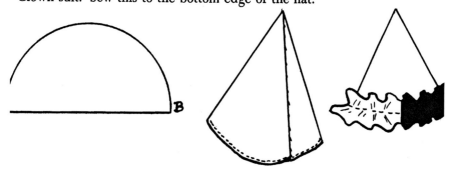

[77]

Puppet and Marionette Costumes

For a hand Puppet, the Clown outfit can be used. Follow the same pattern but use only the top of the suit. Leave it long enough to cover the hand when you work the Puppet.

How to Make the Ballet Dress

The Ballet costume is made of tarlatan. This material is fun to work with as it is stiff net and will make the skirt stand out. Also, it will not ravel and the edges need not be hemmed.

Tarlatan is very thin and transparent, so it is necessary to make a lining for the costume. The material for this should be the same color as the tarlatan—either cotton or silk. This pattern has a romper foundation of waist and tights. The romper waist should be made of tarlatan with a lining of the heavier material.

Cut the romper waist from the lining material. Then using it as a pattern, lay it on your tarlatan and cut a duplicate piece.

The waist of the romper may be cut in one piece by folding the material at the shoulders. (Lay your doll on the material, with the fold at her shoulders, and cut around her.) Cut a low neck and arm holes. Plan the waist so it will fit tight. Cut a slit all the way down the middle of the back.

[78]

The tights are made of the lining material only. They should fit snugly at the waist but may be loose at the leg. Lay your doll on two thicknesses of the material and cut the tights in the pattern illustrated.

When you have cut the waist from both the tarlatan and the lining material, lay one on top of the other with the wrong side of the lining out, and sew close to the edge of the neck and down the back opening. Now separate the two waists. Sew up the side seams of the lining, and then the side seams for the tarlatan—stitching them on the wrong side. Turn the tarlatan waist right side out, and fold the lining inside. You will find that the waist has finished edges everywhere except around the arm holes and the bottom. Turn in the arm hole edges—folding them between the two layers of material—and sew them together.

Sew the side seams of the tights. Then make a hem at the bottom of each leg. Cut two pieces of elastic, long enough to fit around the doll's thigh, and run the elastic through each hem. Pin the ends of the

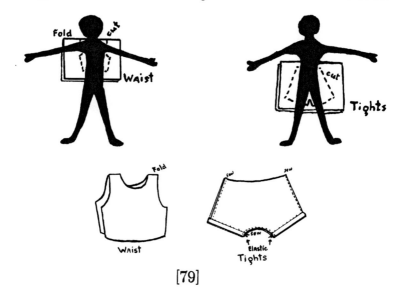

[79]

elastic on the crotch edge. Now stitch the crotch seam of the tights. (This will also fasten the elastic.) Cut a slit down the middle of the back and make a small hem on both edges of this opening.

Put the waist on your doll and pin the pants to the waist—turning the top edge of the tights under. The waist opening and the pants opening should meet. The side seams should come together. After the suit has been pinned all around the waist, take it off the doll and sew along the pinned seam. Sew snaps to the back opening—on the waist and at the top of the tights.

The skirt of the Ballet dress is cut in a straight piece, and very full. There should be only one seam and that comes in the middle of the back. Leave a few inches open at the top for a placket. Cut four or five layers of skirt. When you have sewed up the back seams of each one, turn under the top edge of each skirt, then put them together (one inside the other). Run a gathering thread in the top, gathering all the layers together. Pull up the gathering thread to fit the waist of the tights and sew the layers of skirt to the bottom edge of the waist— where it is attached to the tights.

The more layers of skirt you have, the more the dress will fluff out. Some Ballet dresses are so full they stand out straight from the hips. Do not try to hem the skirt layers. It is not necessary with tarlatan.

CHAPTER THIRTEEN

Dressing the Bride

THIS CHAPTER IS ABOUT the Bride Doll and how to make her dress, veil, and flower bouquet. Use any white silk for the dress—crepe, taffeta, or satin. The veil should be net. For this you can use cotton, or silk-net curtain material. An old curtain usually has enough good material to make a doll's veil. A small piece of buckram will be useful when you are making the crown for the veil. A little lace and a few white beads are also on the list of things you will need.

The Bride's Dress

The bride's dress is cut in seven pieces: the waist—two pieces for the back and one for the front; the skirt—back and front; and two long sleeves. The skirt reaches to the ankles in front, and has a train in the back. The dress opens down the back.

Be sure to measure around the doll correctly when you cut the waist, as the dress should fit snugly at the waistline. When you cut the back of the waist, allow for the back opening. To do this, baste a hem

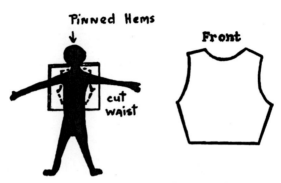

in one edge of both pieces of material, then pin the pieces together—lapping one hem over the other. Lay this pinned section on another piece of material (the piece that will be the front of the waist), and draw the waist pattern around the doll as she lies on the material. Have the pinned hems at the middle of her back—from the neck to the waist.

In cutting the sleeve, make the top A higher than the arm hole in the waist (B), so it will puff a little when it is sewed in.

Cut the skirt full so it will gather around the waist. The back of the skirt is the same length as the front at the side seams, but the train may be cut as long as you like.

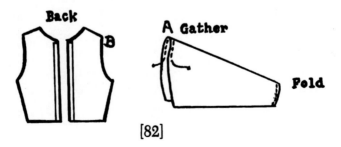

[82]

In sewing the waist pieces together, first stitch the shoulder seams. Then hem the bottom of each sleeve. Next run a gathering thread in the tops of the sleeves and sew them to the arm holes—having the extra fullness come at the shoulders. Make a very narrow hem at the neck, and hem the back opening (which is already basted). Now you are ready to sew up the side seams of the waist. When that has been done, turn under the bottom edge of the waist (all the way around), and baste it—so it will be ready for the skirt.

Before sewing the seams of the skirt, cut an opening a short way down the middle of the back piece C. Make a narrow hem along each edge of this opening. Now sew up the side seams. Run a gathering thread in the top of the front of the skirt, from seam to seam, and pin the skirt to the inside of the waist—at the center front and each side seam. Draw up the gathering thread so that the skirt front fits the waist front. Spread the gathers out evenly and put in more pins to hold the skirt to the waist. Gather up both sides of the back of the skirt to fit both sides of the back of the waist. Spread the gathers out evenly and put in pins to hold them. Now baste around the waist where you have pinned. Then take out the pins and sew the skirt to the waist—sewing close to the turned under edge at the bottom of the waist. Now you can pull out the bastings.

Make a narrow hem around the bottom of the skirt.

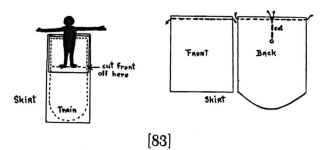

[83]

You are ready to trim the bride's dress. This pattern is for a dress with bead trimming. Perhaps you have a broken string of pearls or small white beads. If so, they are just what you need. Sew them around the neck of the dress, making a design of flowers or snowflakes. The beads should be sewed on one at a time but as close together as you like. Put one or two rows of beads around the waist and at the bottom of each sleeve. A line of them down the back opening will look like buttons. (But fasten the dress with snaps.)

Beads for Trimming

Bead Designs

Front

Back

Train

[84]

The Bride's Veil

To make the bride's veil you must first have some sort of form to use as a crown on which to sew the veil. If you have buckram, make it of that. A piece of starched cloth can be used, but be sure it is really stiff before you cut it. Make this crown big enough to go around the doll's head with enough extra to lap over at the back. Cut it narrow at the back and about an inch wide at the front. (See illustration.) Fit it to the doll's head, sewing it together at the back.

The inside of the crown should be covered with net, and the front of the outside covered with lace. Cut the net veil long enough to reach to the bottom of the dress at the sides, and if the back of the gown has a train, shape the veil to match the train. The veil should be wide enough to make a soft gathering around the back of the crown. Net will not have to be hemmed, but the part that gathers to the crown should be turned under about ½ inch and the stitches taken about ¼ inch from the folded edge—to make a small ruffle around the crown. This should be attached to the back of the buckram, starting just above the doll's ears.

A few beads sewed in the same pattern you used on the dress will be pretty around the front of the crown. Then sew single beads around the back—over the gathered net. Sew each bead on one at a time the same way you sewed them around the neck and sleeves of the dress.

The Bride's Bouquet

A very pretty bouquet can be made from odd pieces of silk in soft pastel shades—blue, pink, lavender, yellow, green. Cut these pieces into circles about half an inch across, and gather up the edges. Sew a bunch of them together and around the bunch gather a piece of white lace. You can also add a few streamers of white ribbon—narrow ribbon—with

Gathering
String

some of the silk flower petals attached to the ends. Sew the bouquet to the waist of the bride's dress, or tie it to her wrist with white ribbon when she is dressed in her bridal gown and veil.

CHAPTER FOURTEEN

Sewing Tricks and Fancy Stitches

Ways to Sew on Buttons

HAVE THE KNOT UNDER THE button and on the right side of the cloth. But in finishing, fasten the thread on the wrong side. Sew through the holes to make a cross or horizontal lines.

Work over a pin so it will not be too tight.
Wind thread around the stitches under the button.

How to Make a Buttonhole

Cut a straight slit in the cloth—making it a little longer than the width of the button to be put through it. Now, using coarse cotton thread, take a small stitch at one end of the slit. Then leaving a long thread to run the length of the hole, take another stitch at the other

[87]

end. Next, make another long stitch on the opposite side of the slit. (Four stitches in all. See illustration.) The next step is to take a few stitches over and over the edges of the hole—overcasting. You are now ready to start your buttonhole stitch. Make the stitches close together and go all around the hole.

How to Sew on Snaps

Be sure the outside of the snap faces the cloth. Before sewing it on, fasten the snap together if you are in doubt about which is the outside. Be careful not to have your thread cross the top of the snap as you sew it to the cloth.

How to Sew on Hooks and Eyes

 Fasten the top as well as the holes of the hook.

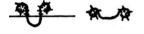 Fasten around the holes of the eyes.

How to Sew on Lace

With the right sides together, overcast the bottom edge of the lace to the edge of the material.

How to Make a Hem

Working on the wrong side, turn the edge of the material over twice—once close to the edge, and then again the width you want the hem. Baste it in place. Now sew the hem on the wrong side. Slant the needle and take a small stitch (a thread or two) close to the hem, and bring the needle up through the edge of the turned down hem.

How to Cut Your Own Bias Binding

The bias strip is cut on the diagonal of the cloth. To find the diagonal, fold the selvage edge back even with the straight edge. (Be sure the edge is straight. Tear it if possible, pull a thread to cut on, or follow the pattern if the cloth has one.)

 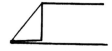 

[89]

How to Sew a Binding

Turn down the long edges of the binding about ¼ inch. Then fold the strip in half lengthwise. Lay this folded strip over the edge to be bound. Baste it in place—being careful not to stretch the material or the binding. Then sew close to the inside edge and be sure the stitches fasten the underside of the binding as well as the top.

SOME FANCY STITCHES

Lazy Daisy Stitch (Figure 1)

Start at the center of the daisy, and bring your needle through the cloth from the back side. Put the needle in the cloth at the center again and take a stitch the size you want the petal. Wrap the thread under the needle point and bring the needle out of the cloth. Put the needle point in the cloth just beyond the end of the petal and take a stitch under the petal to the center of the daisy. Make the other petals the same way.

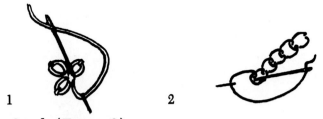

1   2

Chain Stitch (Figure 2)

Bring your needle through the cloth from the back side, then put the needle in the same hole and take a stitch the size you want the link to be. Keep the thread under the point of the needle when you take the stitch. Continue making links the same way—each time putting in the needle inside the end of the last loop.

Feather Stitch

Bring your needle through the cloth from the back side. Now take a small stitch with the thread under the point of the needle. Take another small stitch to the left and above the first stitch, again with the thread under the needle. Continue these stitches, alternating from top to bottom, and moving a little to the left with each stitch.

Cross Stitch

Slant the stitches and begin the work from either direction. Each cross may be made separately, or one may sew a row of thread lines slanting in one direction and then sew the crossed thread lines slanting in the other direction. Be sure to make all the stitches the same length.

Y Stitch

Bring your needle through the cloth from the back side. Put the point of the needle in the cloth again in line with the first hole and a little to the right of it. Bring the point out below the two holes and halfway beween them. Wrap the thread under the point of the needle and pull the needle through the cloth. Then put the needle in the cloth again directly below the last hole and as far away as you want the stitch that forms the bottom of the Y. Pull the needle through the cloth to the back side.

Catch-Stitch

Slant these stitches and work from left to right. Bring your needle through the cloth from the back side—for the bottom of the first cross. Then° put the point of your needle in the cloth a little to the right and above the first hole. Take a stitch, bringing the needle out a little to the left and in line with where the point went in—but not as far to the left as the bottom of the cross. Pull the thread through. Now put the point of the needle in the cloth in line with the bottom of the cross and a little to the right of the top of the cross. Take a stitch, bringing the needle out a little to the left of where it went in. Repeat these directions from°.

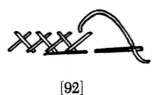

A Dictionary of Sewing Terms

BACK STITCH

BACK STITCH: (Machine stitch)

BASTING

BASTING: Long stitches used to hold two or more pieces of material together. They are not permanent and should be made with fine thread that will not leave holes.

BIAS: Diagonal—across the threads of the cloth.

BIAS

BINDING: A strip (straight or bias) sewed to the edge of the cloth. See Chapter Fourteen.

BLANKET STITCH

BLANKET STITCH

BOX PLEAT: Two folds under the upper folds.

BUTTONHOLE STITCH: See Chapter Fourteen.

BOX PLEAT

CROTCH: The angle between the two legs.

FACING: A separate piece of material, sewed to the edge of a garment and turned back for a finish.

FRENCH SEAM

CROTCH

FRENCH SEAM: Seam is sewed on the right side, and again on wrong. Cut off the material close to the stitching line before making the second stitching.

[93]

GATHER

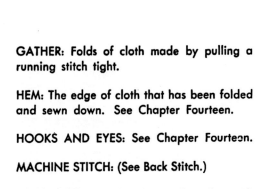

HEM

PINKING

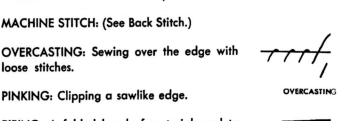

OVERCASTING

PLACKET

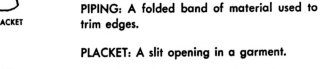

PIPING

PLEAT

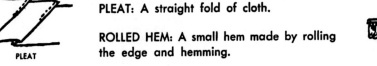

RUCHING

ROLLED HEM

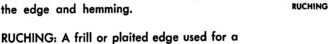

RUNNING STITC

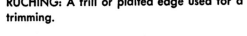

TUCKS

SELVAGE

GATHER: Folds of cloth made by pulling a running stitch tight.

HEM: The edge of cloth that has been folded and sewn down. See Chapter Fourteen.

HOOKS AND EYES: See Chapter Fourteen.

MACHINE STITCH: (See Back Stitch.)

OVERCASTING: Sewing over the edge with loose stitches.

PINKING: Clipping a sawlike edge.

PIPING: A folded band of material used to trim edges.

PLACKET: A slit opening in a garment.

PLEAT: A straight fold of cloth.

ROLLED HEM: A small hem made by rolling the edge and hemming.

RUCHING: A frill or plaited edge used for a trimming.

RUNNING STITCH: Small, even stitches.

SELVAGE: The straight edge of the material that has a store finish so it will not ravel.

SNAPS: See Chapter Fourteen.

TUCKS: Small sewed down pleats.

[94]

Index